A Smile Behind My Mask!

DR NEVILLE HEADLEY DDS

A **COLLECTION** OF **ACTUAL DENTAL** **PATIENT** QUOTATIONS

May the smile you generate reading this book be infectious.

Dr. Neville Headley

Publishing Guidance with Heather Andrews
Book Cover and Layout Design by Lorie Miller Hansen
Digital ePub design and creation by Andrea Cinnamond

ISBN (paperback) 978-1-0688687-1-9
ISBN (hardcover) 978-1-0688687-2-6

First Edition, printed July 2024
DrNevilleHeadley.com

Dedication

Dedicated to my Mom and Dad, Germaine and Randy. They raised six inspiring children and a station wagon full of cousins, nieces, nephews and grandchildren. Our wonderful parents spoke, chatted, informed, negotiated, and conversed with us daily. Many of their quotes made us think but the most memorable ones made us smile... sometimes after they had left the room.

Table of Contents

YOU CAN LEARN SO MUCH JUST LISTENING...

It opens the door to connection and awareness of genuine humour in conversation. My dental patients have been making me smile, behind my mask, for decades. Their spontaneous responses to simple questions or their natural observations have been music to my ears, my smile and my funny bone.

I hope you enjoy and share this compilation of quotations and come to realize a sense of humour has always had a home in my dental surroundings.

meal
mishaps

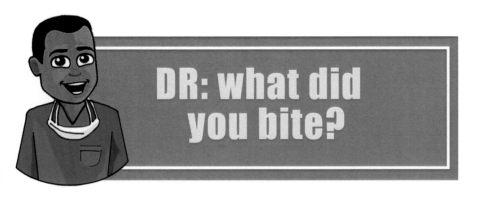

DR: what did you bite?

PATIENT RESPONSES:

"Pistachio shells! I used to love 'em, now I hate them."

"It was terrible. It took out both front fillings. I haven't touched Biscotti for nine years."

"I was eating a cookie and I thought... hmmmm, that's NOT a chocolate chip."

"I chipped these three teeth when I bit into a cinnamon bun that had a fork in it."

"It happened a week ago. Now I have a chip and it's not on my shoulder."

"I was just sitting there and all of a sudden the tooth was loose. Then the brownie did the rest."

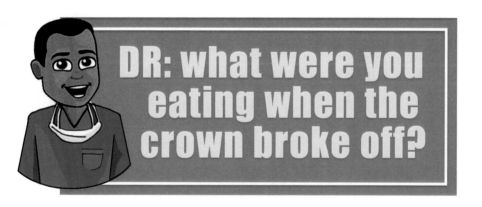

PATIENT RESPONSE:

"A sandwich. It's always something that's not even fun."

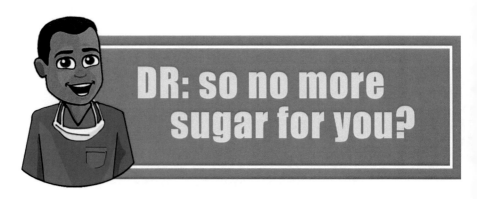

PATIENT RESPONSE:

"No, I'm sweet enough already."

Treasure Chest!

"That impression material almost looks tasty enough to spread on a bagel."

"I was telling the hygienist I'm still trying to figure out who keeps putting red wine and coffee in my mouth!"

The Bow River

> **The urban core of Calgary frames the beauty of the Bow River as it meanders through the inner city.**

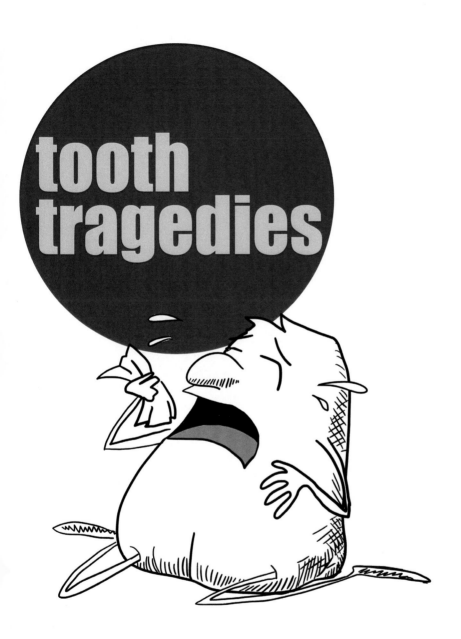

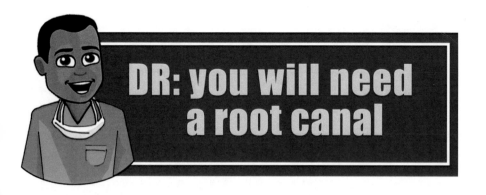

DR: you will need a root canal

PATIENT RESPONSES:

"Well, you can scratch root canal
off my bucket list."

"What could be better for
Christmas than 30° below and
a root canal?"

"I can always pray that the tooth
gets better. I'm not religious
but I can pray."

PATIENT RESPONSE:

"Maybe I need to start searching eHarmony or Bumble to make that happen."

Treasure Chest!

"OOPS... was THE one word you never wanted to hear spoken by the bomb disposal expert, your Doctor, or your Dentist.

"It's the perfect background music for something so nasty. I hate extractions and I hate Nickelback!"

"I hate to say this but nice to see you again."

"Do make sure you pull the right tooth because we don't want to anger the Tooth Fairy."

"I'm so old they didn't use freezing and the drills were on pulleys."

PATIENT RESPONSES:

"I've been told by some very close friends I have a screw loose. But it appears I DO have an implant screw loose."

"If I lose this other front tooth then I can move to Arkansas and fit right in."

"My teeth don't like to leave me. I had one extraction and he had to put his knee on my chest."

DR: i'm going to touch an icicle to your tooth. raise your left hand when you detect the sensation of cold.

PATIENT:

"YOU enjoy doing this, don't you."

DR: how is life with you?

PATIENT:

"It doesn't matter how much yoga
I do, I still clench at night."

DR: is there any pain from those teeth?

PATIENTS:

"Only the anticipatory pain in my wallet."

"There are only two mantras in the
world. One is 'yuck' and one is 'yum'.
The choice is yours."

DR: this denture reline should help with retention

PATIENT:

"Good. I can hardly wait until I can bite people again."

DR: plans for the weekend?

PATIENT:

"Yeah, yoga. And wine. But not at the same time."

DR: i'll sit you up

PATIENT:

"Oh! It's started to snow. Can you lie me back down?"

DR: have you had lunch yet?

PATIENT:

"Why? Are you buying?"

DR: when the blinds are open it can get bright and quite hot in here

PATIENT:

"That's a perfect description of me."

DR: what do you do for recreation??

PATIENT:

"Overtime."

DR: where do you work?

PATIENT:

"In the hospital operating room and I don't want to see YOU there!"

DR: is the tooth sensitive?

PATIENT:

"No. I'M sensitive but not the tooth."

DR: are you prepared to have the tooth removed today?

PATIENTS:

"I wasn't. I thought you were just going to have a look and then read me a bedtime story."

"Is the tooth out already? Excellent! I'll have a Cerveza."

"All the kids sports are paid for so I'm off the hook for a month. I figured I better get this tooth fixed now."

"I wonder when the first tooth in history was pulled and who did the pulling?"

"With the loss of this tooth I may lose some weight. I might come back and ask you to take another one out."

DR: how are you?

PATIENT:

"The pits. I had a toe removed this morning and this molar is aching badly. I wonder how much weight I lost with that toe removal?"

—Reflections on a Second Summer—

" I love to reflect on the enjoyment of my favourite season. "

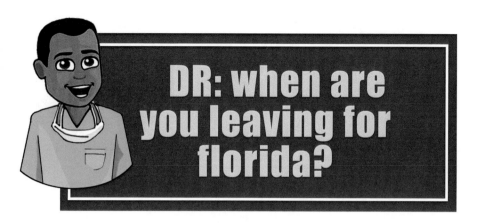

DR: when are you leaving for florida?

PATIENT RESPONSES:

"The next time I get a toothache... seems to be the pattern."

DR: so, how did the crown come off?

PATIENT:

"We were in Costa Rica, we rolled a quad and my buddy fell on my face."

DR: how was your vacation?

PATIENTS:

"It was wonderful. Fourteen hundred dollars for a 19-day cruise. I have to find good travel deals because I drop thousands of dollars every time I come here."

"Machu Picchu was amazing. Japan was tough because of the language. In China I didn't know if I was walking into a restaurant or a mortuary."

"Great, but whenever we'd say we were from Canada they would always ask 'Are you from that place that's always on fire?' "

Fun in The CFB Sun

 With the hatch open on this Chieftain Main Battle Tank it felt like a personalized sunroof.

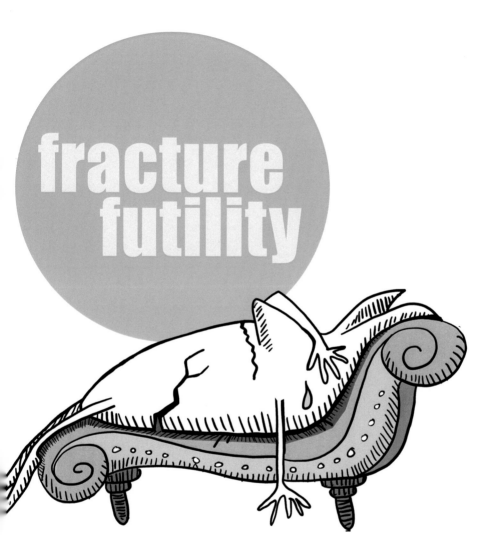

fracture futility

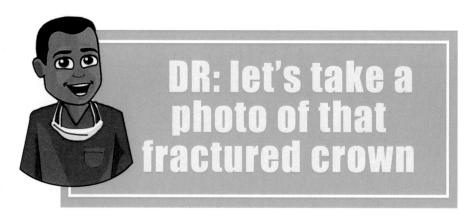

DR: let's take a photo of that fractured crown

PATIENT RESPONSE:

"I never thought of my tooth as a crime scene."

Treasure Chest!

"Thank you for seeing me so quickly. Is this when you use the Gorilla Glue?"

DR: you will need a crown on that molar. are you free this saturday morning?

PATIENT RESPONSE:

"Why are you short of cash?"

DR: are you nervous?

PATIENT:

"My tooth coming out in the impression was my nightmare last night."

DR: how did you originally lose the filling?

PATIENT:

"I was lifting weights and I clean & jerked the bar into my face."

DR: how did you chip that tooth?

PATIENTS:

"It first chipped about ten years ago when I got too aggressive with one of those tomahawk steaks."

"I was looking up and so were my feet when I tripped on the cobblestones and landed face down."

"The tooth broke three months ago. I hope you don't use the same tools I use to break things apart."

"I don't care about my nails. If it's too tight I'm more worried about chipping a tooth when removing the splint."

"I bit into a fig and broke the filling. I just started crying. I was going to get Crazy Glue to put it back in. I may never eat another fig."

"When I was a crazy youth travelling through Switzerland I would open bottles with my front teeth.
Unsurprisingly, the other patrons would fill my table with more beers."

Treasure Chest!

"I tried to get rid of the Valentine candy before Easter, thus the broken tooth."

"We were at a restaurant in Canmore. The first bite into the beautiful steak I ordered ruined the tooth and my appetite."

—A Painted Sunset—

One of many Alberta July sunsets that commands your attention and overwhelms your gaze.

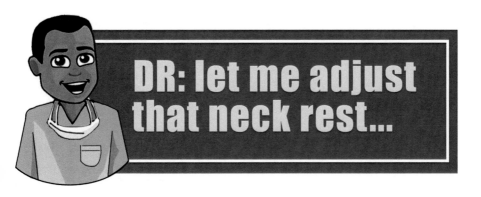

DR: let me adjust that neck rest...

PATIENT RESPONSE:

"Doc, I'm used to a pain in the neck.
I have two daughters."

DR: do you have pets?

PATIENT:

"No, just a 2 and a 4 year old so
we're maxed out."

Treasure Chest!

"I never have any problems falling asleep here in the dental chair. Yet I've slept next to my wife for fifty years and I'm still an insomniac."

"My husband says it's quieter in the house when I have a toothache."

"My husband said he needed an implant to which I replied...
NO teeth NO wife."

"The tooth has bugged me ever since I got pregnant. So I blame it on my husband."

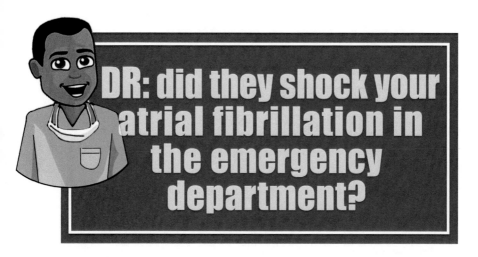

DR: did they shock your atrial fibrillation in the emergency department?

PATIENT RESPONSE:

"Yes. My daughter is training as a nurse and was on duty. There was no waiting. I got quick treatment and the best room."

DR: nothing to worry about

PATIENT:

"I'm pregnant. I don't have any room to worry." ● ● ● ● ● ● ● ●

Treasure Chest!

"I like what you said about my mouth being small but could you tell my wife that."

"I answered my phone while I was waiting. It was my wife telling me we are having company for dinner.... so take your time."

"We've come a long way since I was a kid where my parents choose between a car and braces. We got the car."

"Now I get to go shoe shopping with my wife. I hate going to the dentist but I hate shoe shopping even more."

DR: how was your weekend?

PATIENT:

"Do you want a 15-year old?"

DR: i will prescribe you an antibiotic...

PATIENT:

"Good, because I had some lying around for the dog and I was going to start taking them."

DR: thanks for coming in on short notice!

PATIENT:

"No problem. My father-in-law was a dentist so I know the drill."

DR: while you were on your hike yesterday did you see any wildlife?

PATIENT:

"Just some squirrel tracks and a bunch of school kids."

Treasure Chest!

"There is not a whole lot you can continually blame your parents for....teeth are it."

"My eight-year-old is in the *"scary"* phase. Hiding, as a Zombie Scarecrow, and trying to see how loud he can get Mom to scream."

"I awoke at 4, got up at 5 and had three loads of laundry done by 8. The whole gang is coming home tonight. It's been go, go, go ever since so if I fall asleep it's ME, not you."

Treasure Chest!

"I saw Alabama live when pregnant with my daughter and Neil Diamond when pregnant with my son. Their musical tastes are interestingly, quite varied."

"My daughter was supposed to move in with us but she's living on the mainland in a RV with a boyfriend that I wish the wilderness would swallow up."

"I had two very good husbands and they both died of cancer... but not at the same time."

DR: is your lip still numb? Can you whistle?

PATIENT:

"I'm five—I don't know how to whistle."

DR: how was the climate change play?

PATIENT:

"I was really happy with my son's performance. He was with three other girls but he was the best at depicting floating garbage in the ocean."

DR: did you know that your wife sill has a retained baby tooth and is missing the exact same adult tooth as you?

PATIENT:
"What! I did not know that about her and she does not know that about me. Wow, what are the chances?"

Treasure Chest!

"On the weekend we did a little experiment with Banana Bread French Toast. OMG, it was delicious!"

"I asked my child what he wanted for his birthday. He said a 'vending machine.' I said no! Then he said 'I want a new Mom.'"

"I was considering the porcelain option but my kids want me to have a gold tooth back there."

"I've been told I have a small mouth although my husband will dispute that."

Treasure Chest!

"I never dreamed that one day I'd look forward to and enjoy going on vacation with my quarter horse."

DR: the time flies and we spring forward this weekend

PATIENT:

"Big birthday for me on Saturday. I'll be sixty-five again... for the 25th time."

—The Double Flat Spin—

" A warm up shortly before the Calgary Stampede Promotion Committee's Happy Trails monthly celebration of our western heritage at senior's residences around the city. "

drill
bits

DR: the short acting freezing was used so you will be back to normal in an hour.

PATIENT RESPONSE:

"Define normal?"

DR: try not to do anything that would increase your heart rate.

PATIENT:

"I'm not sure if that means going to work or staying away from work." • • • • • •

Treasure Chest!

"You're placing four implants today. Doc, you know I'd rather be dancing with you!"

"Brushing and flossing is a job that never ends. Well I guess it eventually does, but we don't want to talk about that."

"Using so much sanitizer on my hands has turned me into an alcoholic."

"Are these dark safety glasses so you don't see the tears in my eyes?"

PATIENT RESPONSE:

"That's because I'm lying down. When I stand up I get heavier."

DR: having looked at your x-rays here is what I'm proposing.

PATIENT:

Doc, I don't think we've known each other long enough for you to propose." • • • • • • • • • • • • •

Treasure Chest!

"Doc, you're just the person I want to see... until I HAVE to pay the bill."

"It's been five years Doc and you look younger... but my eyesight is not what it used to be."

"It used to be serious when the gloves came off, but now it's serious when the gloves go on."

"I like being a teacher. The other day I had three kids stay to help clean up but they started playing the piano. I told them I don't have a headache but I'm getting a migraine."

DR: how were the drugs?

PATIENT:

"Great! Can I take some home with me?"

DR: how are you?

PATIENT:

"I'm fine but don't YOU ruin my day."

DR: don't work out for a few days

PATIENT:

"THIS...... THIS does not work out!" · · · · ·

DR: beautiful! (referring to the new x-ray)

PATIENT:

"Thank you Doc. I've been working out."

DR: how did the house painting go?

PATIENT:

"I didn't get to it. I opened a bottle of wine instead."

Treasure Chest!

"I laughed when you pulled my tongue out because it made me feel like livestock."

"The trouble with overhead TVs is you come in the middle of a show and you leave before it's over."

"Have you ever noticed when you run across a group of joggers all the nice people are at the back."

"It's amazing how much teeth move around in the mouth... I guess that's why braces work."

Treasure Chest!

"I still hate dental needles even though I did my own tattoos with a razor blade, a guitar string and a sewing needle."

"I had the option to book for a new crown or enjoy a Caribbean cruise. I leave for Fort Lauderdale in 3 weeks."

"I'm trying to distract myself. Is it working? No, YOU'RE still here."

"Doc, I have to admit your angled glasses are a little unnerving. It feels like I'm being examined by a robot."

DR: how is the freezing?

PATIENT:

"It's good but I'm saying that because I don't want you to give me any more."

DR: bite, tap, tap, tap and grind!

PATIENT:

"That makes me want to dance. I get real stupid when I'm stressed."

DR: how are you doing?

PATIENT:

"Do you want the truth, or the bullshit
I tell everybody else."

DR: would you like a rinse?

PATIENT:

"Water would be nice but a vodka
martini would be better."

Treasure Chest!

"I'm busier than I want to be but I guess that's called job security."

"That didn't hurt a bit, but I haven't got by the front desk yet."

"I'm not going to lie. Dentists make me nervous. Now that I've seen this consent form I'm a little bit more nervous than usual."

"I'm wearing the same colours as you guys, so do I get a discount?"

"Why do you guys make my nose so itchy?"

DR: is there any history of head or neck trauma?

PATIENT:

"When I was younger I fell out of a tree."

DOCTOR: how old were you?

"Twelve years ago when I was seventy."

DR: what did you accomplish this weekend?

PATIENT:

"It was something. I can't remember what... but it was helpful."

Treasure Chest!

"The whole tooth thing is
secondary. I just come here
to watch HGTV."

"That's what happens in your fifties.
You are more excited about
a Saturday appointment with your
dentist than a trip to the bar."

"Whenever I get needles, tears
run down my face, so no
makeup today."

"It's been ten years, but do you still
use the numbing stuff... before
the numbing stuff?"

A SMILE UNDER MY MASK

DR: this will pinch a little

PATIENT:

"Has anyone ever hit you after
that injection?"

DR: how is the numbing?

PATIENT:

"I'm definitely frozen down to here and
up to the eye creases. Is there anything
you can do about them?"

Treasure Chest!

"I've really been looking forward to seeing you and your assistant. Now that I have, can I leave?"

"I'm 93 but I've always said that if I'm coming back I want nice hair and good teeth."

"Wow Doc! Your restoration work is beautiful. I bought a bottle of red wine when I was twenty for my fiftieth birthday, which was last Monday. I think I'll open it tomorrow."

DR: little pinch here...

PATIENT:

"That wasn't a pinch, that was a prick!"

DR: how has your week been?

PATIENT:

"Hectic, but expensive. But at least now I can see through my new windshield."

A Saturn Sky

Some childhood dreams are about smaller things becoming sizeable rewards.

Acknowledgements

I cannot begin to express my thanks to Christy Mercer, my teammate at work, and an inspiration for this and other individual unique projects. Her radiant charisma is coupled with a smile that could melt a glacier and a supportive professionalism that is second to none.

Special thank you to Victoria Givlin, Stephanie Watson, Heather Andrews, Lorie Miller Hansen, Andrea Cinnamond and Mohini Reid whose help was instrumental in the successful continuation of this journey.

About the Author...

DR. NEVILLE HEADLEY CD, B.Sc., DDS

Dr. Neville Headley graduated from the University of Alberta in 1982 and served with the Canadian Armed Forces Dental Services for 20 years, prior to returning to Calgary in 1998.

Currently he enjoys mentoring as much as wisdom teeth removal and placing implants in seven clinic locations.

For the past 24 years Dr. Headley has volunteered on the Calgary Stampede Promotion Committee and prides himself on his dancing (Ballroom, Latin, Country, Line) and western skills (trick roping, gun spinning, whip cracking). He has a passion for both teaching and diversifying the sport of curling.

Extra circular activities have included officiating at two Commonwealth Games, the 1988 Calgary Olympic Games, an extra on the set of *Superman 3*, Las Vegas Nevada Western Stage Props cover model (2018), the

ABOUT THE AUTHOR cont'd...

Calgary greeter (Season 9—Episode 1) for the *Amazing Race Canada*, golf, curling and photography.

His most recent ventures include publishing a first book of photos and quotations, and executive producing the *TANGOMAN* movie and *TANGO THE MUSICAL*, a sizzling stage show featuring world Champion Tango dancers and a Latin Grammy winning orchestra.

Neville has also invented a new surgical dental drill designed to make the removal of wisdom teeth easier.